THE METAPHYSICS
OF THE MODEL

THE METAPHYSICS OF THE MODEL

Values within/toward the Attitude and Approach of Life

Doug Eiderzen

authorHOUSE®

AuthorHouse™
1663 Liberty Drive
Bloomington, IN 47403
www.authorhouse.com
Phone: 1-800-839-8640

First published by AuthorHouse 11/23/2009

ISBN: 978-1-4490-5481-6 (e)
ISBN: 978-1-4490-5480-9 (sc)

Library of Congress Control Number: 2009912679

Printed in the United States of America
Bloomington, Indiana

This book is printed on acid-free paper.

*Unless otherwise indicated, Bible quotations are taken from The
Holy Bible, King James Version of the Bible. Copyright © 1994
by Pradis CD-ROM: Grand Rapids, MI: Zondervan.com.*

CONTENTS

INTRODUCTION

The Metaphysics of the Model is based upon the application, effort, and relevance of two other, yet to be published, manuscripts of methodology for the Model (European American/European). *The Metaphysics of the Model* (European American/Europeanism) will be an approach to life and core to existence for the European American/European and is meshed into the racial culmination of individuality, family, homeland, and spirituality. For our purposes, metaphysics will be the principles (point of view/viewpoint/attitude) to life; that is, a way of living life or, as with a formal definition of metaphysics, "the system of principles underlying a particular study or subject" (Merriam-Webster's, 2004, p. 780). The rudimentary elements which follow will be a basic understanding/essential knowledge to purpose/ rationale. The effort was made (although, not completely successful) not to inundate the writing with a present day montage of examples, as my motivation moves in the fact and direction that I do not desire the writing to be dated by such input. Also, there was the desire to polish each segment to the direct point (crux of the matter) and, yet, move to a general reality of each chapter. So, such an approach will result in each chapter being more concise with more succinct segments presented for the enlightenment to a certain reader. The reader must be the final judge as to the success of the technique. As always, to the European Americans/Europeans there will be the desire and wish for continued achievement to triumph and to our enemies/antagonists the wish for a sustained and never-ending confusion within the realm of chaos.

The book approaches age old concepts in thought and belief and, then, applies these concepts to an everyday approach of life for this unique being, the European American/European. As related to the psyche of said being, hopefully, there will not only be an awareness of spirit but an awakening and arousing of the honor to loyalty mind-set and a pride in the mark of distinction to the viewpoint of admiration. I will call this the general cognitive approach in belonging to the European American/European race (the deductive method to objective). The book focuses on the thought to the application of survival and continuation of life for the Model (European American/European).

The work also centers on the confrontation from without to our race and the battle in conflict from within as to each European American/European individual. The following moves much beyond the classification of country, liberal or conservative, party designation, etc. There are the disciplines of life (the reason for existence/the why in an approach to living). One of these disciplines falls decidedly and directly into the region and area of religion. I would ask the question, as to why any Christian would care or even try to debate with the Devil? There is no need to pray to God for the redemption of Satan. Yet, this is what many of us (European Americans/Europeans) do every day. With that being said, we must view the term Western European as an extremely positive connotation within the origins of our community, family, and nation. Do not be duped into thinking negatively about the term Western European. To our present day America and the Christian religion, we as European American/ Europeans must move beyond past grievances and come together. This can simply be classified as a learning process or experience leading to a mindset (a state of mind/a way of thinking). We must come to terms within our community and within ourselves (the European American/European society and identity). Yes, we must engage the system but we must engage the system from a united consciousness and racially aware standpoint and cohesive cultural point of view. We must engage the system from the perspective of whom we are from a past, present, and future viewpoint (the viewpoint is positive on all accounts). Also, we must engage the system through the perception and perspective of an ultimate philosophy for survival. As to the engagement concerning the system within the dialectic approach, one statement of caution; always respect patience and try to replace emotion with a calm but firm commitment, "he who cannot put his thoughts on ice should not enter into the heat of dispute," (Nietzsche, 2006, p. 158). Our Founding Fathers would demand no less than the above. And, I do believe our Founding Fathers would also remind us that meaningful rhetoric is certainly acceptable but action must be observed by a people and their leaders; this was their exact example. There is nothing worse than to sit back and do nothing presenting a procedure and process that reeks with the stench of failure.

On that basis, we as European Americans/Europeans must realize that we have no one to please but ourselves and that we have no one to apologize to but ourselves. In this approach, there is no guilt, no blame, no shame, no regret, and no remorse. Through this method or attitude, there is no liability, no burden, no humiliation, no responsibility, and no fault to reside within our community or society. So, instead of attacking life, we celebrate it. We move forward. From us, the challenge issued will be toward us: from the whole to the unit and from the unit to the whole. We, as European Americans/ Europeans, should simply state the following to our enemies and their accusations to antagonize, '*and, so*?' If it does not affect or concern us, then, it should not matter to us. For what and to whom should we, as European Americans/Europeans, be contrite? Our enemies do not play at games and neither should we.

As America and the sum of European American/European society and heartland continues the increasingly quick and downward spiral within an existing maelstrom of chaos, it should be realized that when we hit the bottom what is left will splinter and shatter like a heavy glass jar falling to solid concrete. Never forget, when what used to be our America falls, it will fall extremely hard. The catastrophe and disaster without (outside and surrounding) will produce a crisis within each of us; all and everything will be affected. There is no way to determine a time or announce a date of an apocalyptic happening, but the present catalysts for such an event are many. The dilemma to which we face can never be classified as "meaningful coincidences" (Jung, 1973, p. v). The predicaments and actions of ruin, to which the European American/European confronts and must face up to, are deliberate and should be realized by each individual person. Purposeful actions over several decades, and certainly since October 1965 (Immigration and Nationality Act of 1965), can only be construed as most definitely anti-European American/ European. So, let us approach the following with an attitude that '*the die is cast*.' There are two questions, issued with this phenomenon, which are paramount to guidance: How could we (European Americans/ Europeans) have let this happen to our country; the second question and, by far, the most important issue, to answer now, is how we will not only act but visibly react in the pursuance of victory (a racial *modus operandi* leading to a complete racial *modus vivendi*)? The phenomenon moves beyond causality, for cause and effect must react on each other as an awareness (happening) or as Hobbes states, "Consciousness comes after motion as its effect" (1989, p. 237-238). However, within the metaphysics of European American/ Europeanism, racial awareness is readily present through an impression, sense, value, and worth. "We must conclude that besides the connection between cause and effect there is another factor in nature which expresses itself in the arrangement of events and appears to us as meaning" (Jung, 1973, p. 69). Now, intuitive decision making must move to show a realization and achievement in order to exhibit meaning (consequence of value). A positive, tangible endeavor must move to not only demonstrate itself but implant itself. Therefore, time is but a location in the phenomenon of racial reality; so, time only provides a place for the intuitive and the creative to function and take form.

In an example to actuality, within the present political process of our country, the following happens to be reality (whether an action is unlawful or illegal never comes into play as such is overshadowed by a sanctimonious thought of right and wrong): The Hispanic politician is for the best interest of and represents the Latino/ Mexican person; the Black politician is for the best interest of and represents the Black/African person; the Jewish politician is for the best interest of and represents the Jewish/Hebrew person, etcetera, etcetera, etc. Now, the White politician (and this is why I take issue with the term *White* for such is not an acceptable, an accurate, or a distinct designation) moves to represent the welfare and betterment of the above/other races to the detriment of his or her own race. And, at the expense of his or her race, the White politician disregards his or her race with a callous and uncaring attitude of joyously and ceremoniously indulging in the future eradication of such. The expression of being extremely foolish sums up the White politician in this day and age. We (European Americans/Europeans) have been given the choice of quick eradication or slow eradication; let us choose neither. Also, let us remember these past and present day Benedict Arnolds and their associates.

In reference to the Immigration and Nationality Act of 1965, who decided that America (our country) should not remain or continue to be a European American/ European nation? Who decided that America should adopt an anti-European American/European philosophy and that our people should receive the brunt and burden of such a viewpoint with its costly agenda? Who are these traitors and misfits and how did they, not only become to be in our country, but move into the controlling sphere of influence within our nation? There is, simply, no way of determining how many European American/European individuals have been and continue to be adversely and harmfully affected by the abomination of this particular act of treason. Again, purposeful actions over several decades, and certainly since October 1965 (Immigration and Nationality Act of 1965), can only be construed as most definitely anti-European American/European. So, it may be correctly stated that the many establishments of government and its spin-off units have been engaged in a *de facto* war with the European American/European for several decades. Again, there is no way of determining how many European American/European individuals have been and continue to be detrimentally and negatively affected by the abomination of this particular act of treason (Immigration and Nationality Act of 1965).

Since that time of infamy, trust has dissolved for the government and, to a great extent, much that it represents; with good reason, the racially conscious European American/European happens to be very doubtful (wary) and very distrustful (suspicious) of the government, its agencies, and its dubious actions.

The politicians who now seek office and operate the government simply cannot be trusted for the betterment of the European American/European. A question and inquiry of point: Should the country of Mexico move away from its racial core? No. Should the country of Japan move away from its racial core? No. Should the country of China move away from its racial core? No. And, so, again and again the essence of the above question may be asked in regard to a country and its people. Now, should the country of America, the country of Canada, the country of Australia, countries of Europe, and other countries of Western origin move away from the racial core of European American/European? Every American government entity, Canadian government entity, Australian government entity, most every European government entity, and the rest, etc. will adamantly say, yes. And, many non-European American/non-European/non-Occidental countries will, also, say, yes. Now, should we trust our elected officials? No. There is an attack upon our culture and our Christian religion and all that is European American/European.

With regard to voting, there is an old thought to consideration that simply states if a person does not vote then he or she, actually, does not have the right to criticize his or her government. I say, by all means, vote: vote for paralysis on the left side of the body or vote for paralysis on the right side of the body, vote for cancer on the left side of the brain or vote for cancer on the right side of the brain, vote for a stroke affecting the left side of the body or vote for a stroke affecting the right side of the body, etcetera, etcetera, etc. Applying the above analogy, death, or a physical and mental state worse than death, is a definite given. For the European American/ European in our present America, such has become the fundamental nature of voting and all that goes with it. At this stage, the person fretting, worrying, and wondering about whether candidate A defeats candidate B, may be compared to the person fretting, worrying, and wondering whether he or she has left the bath tub water running on the Titanic. Regardless, of whom wins an election, the results and consequences are equally as tragic for the European American/European.

Now, I will interject the following about the ballot. Until we have a *one within our own* statesman or stateswoman who unashamedly, and in all regards, is completely for and totally supports the European American/European, the process of voting is null and void not to mention useless; and, in that respect, I would <u>not</u> recommend the holding of one's breath for such a person to come about soon. For the European American/European, the classic example of a worthless participation in the voting process would be the United States Presidential Election of 2008.

With the above being said, we (European Americans/ Europeans) must carefully and painstakingly examine any war, police action, clash to confrontation, etc. undertaken by this government; it may be, as a racially aware people, we should desire and want to boycott or abort any and all political warfare involvement. We should not be duped and deceived into the willing participation as to some useless, meaningless, and senseless war. It would do well for the present day Agamemnons to understand this, "every army has its breaking point" (Strauss, 2006, p. 110). It goes to reason, the elements making up a fighting force and the elements backing such a force do also have a threshold of breakdown. Therefore, should the partaking in such a police action, war, etc. help to eradicate or eliminate our race, through any reason, then such association must be refused and profusely rejected. No more will we be deceived and misinformed into sending the European American/European son and daughter into the pointless conflict or the trumped-up war for someone else and his or her interests (the person/individual other than our own). Why should the European American/European son and daughter be required or expected to fight and to die for an institution of government from which he and she has long since been separated (i.e., a government which adamantly and openly moves against the European American/European and disagrees with said being in awareness, view, and application; a government which moves to be ecstatic in the suppression of the European American/European; and, a government which through policy and appointment hopes to eliminate the European American/European from his and her country)? We must take the following statement to heart and soul: <u>There will be no more fraternal wars or conflicts with our brotherhood</u>. We must examine all issues from the perspective of our European American/European culture and heritage. This is simply the application of racial consciousness to significance and worth. "Where meaning prevails, order results" (Jung, 1973, p. 72).

For our (European American/European) purposes to terminology, let us substitute the term *conflict to action* in the place of *war*; for, war is <u>not</u> an all encompassing endeavor with regard to the disciplines of life and often ends as suddenly as it starts. For our rationale, conflict to action involves the disciplines of life and affirms to reassert and again avow through acknowledgement, establishment, achievement, and the learning process. The powers that be may play at war, but the conflict to action is constant. It could be said that war acts and thrives on emotion while conflict to action is synonymous with commitment to a way of life. Conflict to action involves an all encompassing struggle to survive and must be, within its scope and capacity, perpetual; as such, it begins with affect (influence to shape) and moves to effect (production of a result) with purpose to deed/movement parallel and equal to both. Conflict to action carries with it a time evolvement (evolution to advancement within knowledge to culture) in progress to purpose and progression to accomplishment. Conflict to action is a learning experience. With the above being said I shall make the statement that there is, definitely, nothing wrong (in regard to the conflict to action) concerning the concept of an ideological man at arms or the perception of ideology in guidance within the actions of the warrior. Conflict to action happens to be the human will itself, or the power of the will; the power of the will manifests itself with direction in the evolution to purpose (reasons to/at objective). We have been engaged in a conflict to action, within some form and within some fashion, since before the beginning of egalitarianism (and all that such institutes and brings into being) concerning our country and our worldly society/culture. There are two entities that are fair game and open season for ridicule, mockery, scorn, contempt, disrespect, and hate: Christianity and Europeanism. Now, would the conflict to action involve, necessitate, and entail a type of hallowed battle and sacred commitment by European American/European men and women? The answer would most definitely be, yes. Our conflict to action is to be given birth within the concept of race, tribal mindset, and ethnic religion and not of the nationalistic war; our conflict to action must be viewed as progression or as a transformation. We as European Americans/Europeans should view with optimism and confidence the stage which has been set before us; all reconfirms.

We are European Americans/Europeans. Concerning this description, we need to be more explicit and uninhibited and less implied and inhibited. The designation of *European Americans* defines our present unique heritage. The designation of *Europeans* defines both our historical and present unique worldly brotherhood. Perhaps, the best motivation for adhering to the uniqueness of our European culture is the fact that we are surrounded by predators and, actually, always have been. This brings into reality the issue of present survival leading to future existence. So, we are <u>not</u> simply Whites, non-Hispanic Whites, Other, etc. We will be referred to as European Americans/Europeans which is what our Founding Fathers were. Being European American/European is a very personal designation and unique classification. It is absolutely mandatory that we claim this designation. We must unequivocally adhere to this title, identity, and description. Such a designation will hold many individuals consciously accountable. The European American/European definition to classification is, certainly, necessary because of its conclusiveness and cohesiveness. The term *Euro-Americaneuropeanism* is synonymous with Nordic tribes, Nordic racial stock, and Nordic sub-racial stock. Euro-Americaneuropeanism is one and the same with the Foundering Fathers and their concepts to existence. Thus, we refer to our term European as all encompassing. The term Euro-Americaneuropeanism should be coined as a bold expression of worldly brotherhood within the temporal and the spiritual for our folk (race, ethnicity, culture, etc.) (Kemp, 2006, chap. 1 and 5). We should live life as European Americans/Europeans.

ABOUT THE AUTHOR

Mr. Douglas Eiderzen has been affiliated and involved in business and building maintenance for many years. Mr. Eiderzen holds qualifications and licenses in several states and has completed assignments in other related fields.

PREFACE

For the teacher/educator/professor/mentor/parent/ child, the following should be incorporated within each lesson to application in some form. There should be a teaching of that which accomplishes and, then, an application of each. Each lesson as to subject application (history, mathematics, English, science, etc.) should contain an introduction, any administrative elements, task of learning, re-teach, and conclusion to include that which has been learned. Rudiments and essentials of the following must be integrated into each teaching strategy and method. With this in mind, the metaphysics of the European American/European child will be established and brought forward. The following should be incorporated within a precise rule to the attitude and direction for the impact and relationship/bond of life. The connection of the unit to the family and the family existence adhering to a responsibility must be constantly reinforced (this cannot be emphasized enough). Thus, all directs itself for the European American/European and his or her survival and continuation in the awareness of life (intellect and morality to commitment and accomplishment).

CHAPTER 1:
WHAT IS THE NATURE
OF THE UNIVERSE

The universe is the European American/European man's and woman's nature for existence (mental and physical). The universe is the binding tie for racial continuation and racial reason of being (the culmination/coming together). Such is the racial past, racial present, and racial future within the universe. The approach for us to our universe is ad-infinitum. As the fresh, cool, mountain air is in motion, the individual is not able of breathe to take in the same air again, yet the infinite flow exists in a melody of thought. This melody of thought is our European American/European racial thought (the racial thought of being). We would say as European American/European racialists the universe was made for us, for are we not here? Racial application is not only our protection from certain negative elements, located and active in the universe, but our reason for existence: the surrounding force. The nature of the universe must be racial accomplishment as such has been within our European psyche from the beginning. Thus, Euro-Americaneuropeanism exists as the clean air of race. And, within the universe why were so many gifts bestowed upon the European American/European being? Such was the unique and distinct blessing as to the leading of one through the endless voids of space; the odyssey of the American European/European is racial reality/identity and the intuitive of being. Within the creation, our universe will be a racial frame of mind applied to a definitive scope in sequence (the infinite journey) for the European American/European child of tribal consciousness. We are to become racial thinkers surrounded by this universe; so, our universe and our creative intelligence, our perception and our intuitive knowledge should unfold and lay exposed to us. "But it is a direct and intuitive knowledge that cannot be reasoned away or arrived at by reasoning; a knowledge that, just because it is not abstract, cannot be communicated, but must dawn on each of us. It therefore finds its real and adequate expression not in words, but simply and solely in deeds, in conduct, in the course of a man's life," (Schopenhauer, 1969, p. 370). This must be taught to our child within his or her thoughts/perceptions and actions/applications. For us, the entity of identity or Model is the substance to being of our European American/European race. Surrounded by the universe, our past, present, and future has, is, and will be our folk (Euro-Americaneuropeanism). The unlimited nature of our universe is our racial being to concept and perception.

CHAPTER 2:
WHAT IS MAN'S PLACE
IN THE UNIVERSE

As we discussed the nature of the universe to the <u>outward approach</u>, the element of man's place in the universe delves into the <u>inward approach</u>. We approach the engagement of the universe and the application of all to our racial philosophy/racial ideas of life: the racial being of himself or herself (the unit) and the belonging to his or her European American/European race (the whole). What is the pure European American/European: Such is the racially aware individual which possesses and cleaves to an applied reason for racial existence within his or her European American/European ethnic group (tribe). This is the European American/European incentive and rationale to purpose. Without this applied racial reasoning, something will always be amiss within that person's existence as to the daily functioning in his or her universe. I would further state that the complete, inner functioning of the Model (progressive European American/European being) would include and encompass the individual, the temporal, and the spiritual; the accomplished state of mind within our universe forming unity.

Man's place in the universe begins with conception and so, the beginning. Jeremiah 1:5 in the Holy Bible, King James Version (1994) states, "Before I formed thee in the belly I knew thee; and before thou camest forth out of the womb I sanctified thee." So, there is the conception leading to birth moving forward to childhood and then to an age of accountability. It would do well for the European American/European individual to employ the above with order, strictness to obedience, and self-control. To employ all of the above will lead to responsibility and discipline. Then, all else that comes with responsibility and discipline will be bestowed upon the European American/European man and woman.

The nature of the universe does not exemplify freedom; the nature of the universe exemplifies order and discipline. Within the European American/European universe the thought of class objective must be replaced with the order and application of discipline and the total assimilation of the will and the objective. The above applications and ideas will be the center of the European American/European child's universe (the self-determination of racial thinking/the racial cognizance of enduring thought). The mindset of the European American/European child will be established in the core of the Model which is to be attained and derived within the sanctity and purity of his or her own race; thus, the total being as to himself or herself existing and functioning within the universe.

CHAPTER 3:
WHAT IS GOOD AND EVIL

The end will always justify the means to us/for us within accomplishment. The objectivity, of good and evil, is not necessarily an ethical or moral approach but an approach to racial completeness through racial awareness. The dependence on an efficient and an effective method to accomplish the objective will lead to a type of disciplined independence in life. The judgment which alludes to and defines the idea of morality is contingent on the milieu (setting, surroundings, etc.) or situation of outcome. Thus, morality is subjective, even selective, and left to perception. So, *outcome* (for our intentions the accomplished act or realization of purpose), itself, is defined by the achievement of goals to the betterment of racial awareness and racial completeness. Pity may be both provisional and permanent depending to whom the recipient happens to be. Pity is the result of an on the spot observance or recollection of circumstances and does play on the emotion of the receiver and/or giver. Pity often has no value but to weaken and diminish the will with the fostering or giving way/in to hesitation. Pity accomplishes absolutely nothing. Nietzsche (2006) stated, "La Rochefoucauld assuredly hits the nail on the head when he warns all sensible people against pity, when he advises them to leave that to those orders of the people who have need of passion (because it is not ruled by reason)…weakens the soul" (p. 45).

The understanding and acceptance of the two concepts of brutality and cruelty should be addressed and focused upon at this point. Brutality (brutality with regard to/of compassion/sensitivity [non-emotion]) is simply the form of accomplishment to goal or plan. There is nothing evil in brutality. To be brutal is in harmony with nature and holds no pity. Cruelty (cruelty with regard to/of non-compassion/insensitivity [emotion]) achieves nothing and promotes no productivity. To be cruel is not in harmony with nature and, eventually, gives way to pity. There is nothing good in cruelty. These two concepts have been addressed in brevity. For us, cruelty is the antithesis of brutality.

The stability and harmony within one's self (to be the will), the chain of command (to accept the directives), and the eugenics to purpose (producing the Model child) will juxtaposition the nature of good and evil.

Good and evil will always be judged within the justification and confines of racial commitment concerning the racially aware person (European American/European). Therefore, one will have the following classic example. In Matthew 22:21 of the Holy Bible (1994), it was stated, "Then saith He [Christ] unto them, Render therefore unto Caesar the things which are Caesar's; and unto God the things that are God's." Within the racial juxtaposition of good and evil, an ongoing application is secondary and may even be termed frivolous and inconsequential to said monumental purpose. We, as European Americans/Europeans, should pursue a type of racial vanity, ethnic narcissism, and cultural egotism. Our children must not let the eddies of the day's perceived morality pull them into the whirlpool of groundless ethics and anti-racial (anti-European American/European) morals. So, we should take heed and be wary of those individuals who conjure up to define the perceived good and the perceived evil by definitions of worldly influence outside of our culture and ethnicity.

The European American/European child must be schooled in becoming a racially complete individual who must be responsible, in control of himself or herself, and steadfast. Such a racial Model becomes the measure of good and evil. The Model, as such, is continuous, unremitting, and unrelenting within his or her actions, needs, and wishes. The above approach is quite Christian and, with this being said, victory, triumph, success, etc. are not to be an end in itself but an ongoing endeavor to commitment within the child leading and moving to adulthood. The child learns to have healthy and good racial objectives to guide his or her purpose. The idea of doing the minor evil to achieve the larger good is of no concern to us because such a statement has no relevance or application. The same would be true of fairness and trust, as these terms would be held to a different set of standards, values, approaches, and disciplines. Our etiquette is created by us and for us within the application of the temporal and the spiritual. There will be no fear in our reasoning.

CHAPTER 4:
WHAT IS THE
NATURE OF GOD

While the nature of God happens to be personal to each individual, the following are concepts of thought for contemplation by the European American/European. Justifiably, the individual may feel and believe that a human only knows or comprehends what he or she may or can experience (Frost, 1989, chap. 10).

If God is to be one and unchangeable then, He will be the source to the sustaining of the individual within his or her race and, if such is the case, then, God did create and will the European American/European as His blessing. God will provide and give us our Valhalla; essentially, such has already happened. As science seeks to prove, God rewards faith. How can we as a racially aware people be so very blessed and yet hated? It would behoove us to remember, what Christ said in John 15:18-19 the Holy Bible (1994), "If the world hate you, ye know that it hated me before it hated you. If ye were of the world, the world would love his own: but because ye are not of the world, but I have chosen you out of the world, therefore the world hateth you". So, why should we be surprised when we are hated? To us, the *why* has already been explained. This being said, one must appreciate himself or herself and identify with his or her own race/people. The person must inundate himself or herself to be within his or her racial need. This comes from racial belonging. More than ever before, we need to move away from the acceptable twist/ploy (the ruse of multiracial exaggeration at its finest) and move toward the actual application/purpose (what is natural and within one's own). Realization that dealing with those that are not our own will produce uneasy coalitions and associations, we would be wise to avoid unnatural alliances for no good can come from such.

The question may be asked, as to whom will be in Heaven? An acceptable answer might be to leave unto God, God's judgment. The European American/European child must be exposed to the existence of faith and knowledge and this may be accomplished from the secular approach or from the approach of belief in God (Supreme Being/Creator) or from the approach of belief in Jesus Christ/Christianity. The European American/European child must be instructed to pursue discipline (and that which is right for him or her within racial strictness, ethnic closeness, cultural faithfulness, etc.) as compared to a narrow and solid road surrounded by fog, marsh and slime, and the realm of darkness. Racial discipline, for the European American/European child, certainly, includes the interlocking and the interconnecting of the temporal and the spiritual. The child through the acceptability of his or her cultural philosophy, ethos, mores, and complete nation will adapt a positive and dogmatic viewpoint toward his or her race. Such is simply meant to be blessed by God. So, God, certainly, is self-preservation.

Supplement/Addendum:

With the conception and/or acceptance of the Trinity (Father, Son, and Holy Spirit), these share and reveal the nature of the Father. Of all the passages within the New Testament, that they despise, none inspires more hatred and brings to bear more contempt than the proclamation, from the Holy Bible (1994), "Lord, we know not whither thou goest; and how can we know the way?

Jesus saith unto him, I am the way, the truth, and the life: no man cometh unto the Father, but by me. If ye had known me, ye should have known my Father also: and from henceforth ye know him, and have seen him" (John 14: 5-7).

There has never been a more successful nurturing and flourishing of life than when there was the coming together of Christianity and the European American/ European. The two combined represent raw power: For all is conquered within life and death for within this acceptance to commitment (mindset) there has been, is, and will be the consummation of all. Within the Holy Bible (1994), it is stated in Revelations 1:8, "I am Alpha and Omega, the beginning and the ending, saith the Lord, which is, and which was, and which is to come, the Almighty."

The time has come when the European American/ European Christian should arise and demand that which has been specified/prearranged and established/ instituted for him or her (to be given ad-infinitum). <u>God never promised us it would be easy and such happens to be the endurances of life</u>. With this being stated, we must accept the fact that life will not be easy for the European American/European child. The pursuit to victory is never easy and, at times, may be quite grueling both mentally and physically. True victory is demanding and costly, because total commitment is required and such necessitates sacrifice, trust, and faith. So, precise and absolute preparation is paramount and the approach to our metaphysics of life must become reality for us. I would state imperatively, Christianity has been diluted and dulled by the religious frauds, charlatans, ashamed regret expressionists, and our racial enemies. Instead of studying the Holy Scriptures in depth/deeply, most organized religious bodies are more attuned to politically correct social enterprises; such may be considered apathetic and tepid. The Holy Bible (1994), states in Revelation 3:15-17, "I know thy works, that thou art neither cold nor hot: I would thou wert cold or hot. So then because thou art lukewarm, and neither cold nor hot, I will spew thee out of my mouth. Because thou sayest, I am rich, and increased with goods, and have need of nothing; and knowest not that thou art wretched, and miserable, and poor, and blind, and naked."

Understand this. There is absolutely no statement in the New Testament which asks a person to give up or forgo or relinquish his or her race. European American/ European virtue is in the uniqueness of self (the eugenics of being). The child must unapologetically and unashamedly discover or rediscover the greatness of his or her religion and his or her race (the two, most definitely, do coincide). With this being said, and as a relation to this, we have been given an effeminate style and slanted approach to Christianity; nothing is further from the truth. One reminder: This is the belief that conquered the Holy Land through the Crusades and this is the belief that compelled our people to dominate many areas of life to existence for the betterment of European Americans/Europeans and this is the belief which triumphs over death. Now, there is no need to reinvent an approach to Christianity. We, as European Americans/Europeans, just need to reread the documents and statements from our racial perspective. This is how we should interpret the Holy Scriptures. For many European American/European individuals, the race goes hand in hand with the religious belief; both are sacred and precious. An extremely important note: <u>There are simply too many similarities between Christianity and the European American/European for such to be a coincidence.</u> It is very difficult to separate the two (the individual and the belief and the temporal and the spiritual). As the European American/European embraces Christianity within his or her life to total victory there is the complete conquering and defeating of death. We have been given a powerful and infinite approach to the Spirit.

CHAPTER 5:
THE QUESTION OF FATE
VERSES FREE WILL

The European American/European child must adopt the attitude that everything which he or she desires and wishes is provided within the temporal area/arena; the European American/European child must adopt the attitude that everything which he or she desires and wishes is provided within the spiritual area/arena: Both of these areas belong to/are within us. Fate tends to fetter the European American/European child while free will challenges the being to the core of his or her existence (that which is within being guided by the temporal and the spiritual). Our future is now, and let us not worry about the prophesies of tomorrow. It is always prudent to anticipate but, anticipation should require appropriate action. So, we should not necessarily ponder and want to know what will take place day after tomorrow to the point of wondering and conjuring up thoughts about fate. "Such prophesies shaped many of the stories in Greek myth, for both gods and humans wanted to know the future" (Parker & Stanton, 2003, p. 45).

The best way to predict the future is with the preparation of today; and, therein rests our quest and mission. The European American/European child will have crucial choices which must be correctly made for his or her race. There are the major choices, within a lifetime, which probably amount to four or five decisions and the minor choices which occur/happen/take place everyday. Both the major choices and the minor choices are directed by the crucial choices of racial concern. Fate is left to the gods where as free will belongs to the actions of man (Euro-Americaneuropeanism). What the gods may know, man accomplishes. Fate will focus on the past and as the present becomes such; free will is a compulsion of the spirit to focus on the future. The future should be reserved for accomplishment, achievement, and success through realization derived from and as a result of present actions. Case in point regarding reason: Simply observe what the European American/European individual has achieved, is achieving, and will achieve. Conviction and devotion and knowledge and realization are actually inseparable and always together for the European American/European. This will be transferred and conveyed to the child. Such is the reality of free will to be exhibited within the European American/European child. Most certainly, free will does incorporate emotion but all must be a controlled emotion for the betterment of the European American/European race. In essence, there must be the conquering of passions for the one combined consequential dedication to be secured and united: reason of race, racial existence, and racial solidarity. Such must incorporate the choice of free will to extend or continue into racial knowledge. Free will decisions are to be made and racial knowledge should guide all commitments to decisiveness in determination. The decision focusing upon and incorporating the act of free will must depend on the intellect. The consequence to summation, of free will, is then built with empirical study forming/derived from the intellect (e.g., observed, pragmatic, and realistic research) which is determined by its racial history, racial precedent, and racial reason. For the European American/European individual and child, this is the power of the will. Let us <u>not</u> worry about tempting fate. Let us engage in racial creative thinking and let us begin the process of creating lasting new memories.

CHAPTER 6:
THE QUESTION OF THE
SOUL AND IMMORTALITY

Although that called death will, eventually, show itself by definition to the European American/ European, the living of that unique being must not be forgotten by those that remain: The substance of the being, contained by the temporal and the spiritual, will depart the clay. As related to essence, is this not the respect which comes with honor to loyalty? This honor to loyalty must be as keen within the self as outside the self. Should not the soul be identified with intellect and/or the thought of accountability and faith? And, should not the intellect, most assuredly, be identified within one's own? The soul of the European American/ European has the power of knowledge and certainty and past realization. Such has, is, and will be the actuality of thought concerning race within the European American/ European child. There is reason and there is purpose, one can accomplish through experience and creative thinking and one can believe through faith. The person will be at one point through this experience but will be at the next point through faith (the continuous meshing and incessant interconnecting of the tangible and the intangible).

Does the soul exist? Yes. Does immortality exist? Yes. However, there must be reinforcement with information and faith to be acknowledged. The European American/ European child must understand that the realities of life will produce pain, hurt, grief, loss, etc; the European American/European child must understand that the realities of life will produce pleasure, peace, joy, victory, etc. The soul will endure with the harmony of belonging to one's own and through the faith and assurance of immortality. This is the power of the will, of the European American/European individual, in honor to loyalty. What we are, and all that we will be, comes from our racial culture and our faith.

Supplement/addendum:

An observation to what is called the soul of the person shows acceptance to function. If the soul may be functional to harmony then such must be within its ethnic and cultural state to belief. This observation, I believe, shows a continuity and link of a past as guidance, within the present, leading to a future. If the soul shows non-harmony, then I believe there may be the worthless attempt to justify, and even deify, worldly possessions and the accumulation of more and more at whatever price. So, different motivations are present but non-functional to a lasting belief; within this assumption, there is very little happiness leading to contentment. The functional soul adheres to the following: In the Holy Bible, (1994) John 6:35 states, "And Jesus said unto them, I am the bread of life: he that cometh to me shall never hunger; and he that believeth on me shall never thirst." And, another reference, John 4:13-14 the Holy Bible, (1994) Jesus answered, "and said unto her, Whosoever drinketh of this water shall thirst again: But whosoever drinketh of the water that I shall give him shall never thirst; but the water that I shall give him shall be in him a well of water springing up into everlasting life."

Now, the dysfunctional soul of man keeps producing the dysfunctional family which produces the dysfunctional community which produces the dysfunctional society which produces the dysfunctional government. So, there is the realm of a totally dysfunctional state of existence; any thought or action outside this realm of absurdity and idiocy is defined as radical by the powers that be. The dysfunctional government reflects the dysfunctional society as to its actions. This societal labyrinth equals lunacy as it keeps going back to the same fountain over and over again but gaining absolutely nothing (quenching no thirst). "True, if quality of intellect could be made up for by quantity, it might be worth while to live even in the great world; but, unfortunately, a hundred fools together will not make one wise man" (Schopenhauer, 2004, p. 15).

CHAPTER 7:
THE QUESTION OF MAN
AND THE STATE

The more homogeneous the state remains to the race of its beginning ethnic group, then, the more revered the state becomes and remains to said ethnic group. The beginning, established race considers loyalty to the state/nation, certainly, a top priority as long as the state/nation is loyal, faithful, and trustworthy to the beginning ethnic group (the traditional being/pure citizenry [those of the Founding Fathers]). However, the more the state moves away, for whatever reason, from the above approach/commitment the more the state will become ill-intended to, for, and toward the original ethnic group and, likewise, the more the original ethnic group will despise and loathe the state and what it has become. The following will apply to the overall perception of the original ethnic group: If the standard of past life has proven and was perceived to be much better than the standard of present life then the state is, actually, looked down upon with a certain contempt and becomes quite distrusted and despised. In this situation the standard may be defined as the original ethnic group's values, past history, and convictions. The synonym for the term state is government.

The state should be racial in existence. If, in general, man is a gregarious being then the individual should, and would, be most expressive and sociable and productive in the company of his or her own racial group (the group will not flourish without the racially conscious person and the person will not bloom to full potential without the racially aware group). The state should always take the responsibility for individual actions and truly, the individual should take the responsibility of state actions (a given within this type of racially political environment). Such should in fact be a certainty regardless of the situation as long as both entities are proceeding for the betterment (both short term and long term application) of the European American/ European (the traditional being/pure citizenry [those of the Founding Fathers]). The state should be racial in the support and continuation of our way of life (the standards thereof). The more racial his or her state becomes the far better the European American/European adjusts. In essence, the European American/European individual and the racial state should exist and move within each other. With the implementation of this concept, the idea of laissez faire simply becomes reality. However, be not fooled, pure and uncontrolled freedom does nothing more than create an anomie leading the rot to riot and a rioting of the rot, etcetera, etcetera, etc. Within the correct, proper, and appropriately controlled racial state (existence to and for the European American/European) the product of synthesis and benevolence leads to a type of ethnic camaraderie and cultural motivation within the individual.

It is well worth mentioning that one will have problems living in another's state (political country/nation/land/territory). This is reality as proof positive and, thus, most obvious will be the application in the functioning of the First Amendment (Freedom of religion, speech, press, assembly and petition), Second Amendment (the individual's right to keep and bear arms), Fifth Amendment (Not to be a witness against ones self, tried for the same crime twice, due process of the law, private property taken for public use), Sixth Amendment (Right to a speedy trail by jury, confronted by witnesses, assistance of counsel for defense), Seventh Amendment (Right to a jury trial), and Eighth Amendment (excessive fines, cruel and unjust punishment).

For example, with reference to the 2nd Amendment, the racial makeup in certain lands and areas cannot control, or mentally cope with, and manage the function concerning the legal ownership of firearms and/or weaponry. Very often, and in many instances, such deals with the mental maturity, mental motivation, rational makeup, and capable intelligence of a member within a society. Is the adopted unit (the non-European American/European) capable or will such simply be a burden on the state and the dominate society? The most

Doug Eiderzen

important examination of issue will be the price paid by the dominate society as the adopted unit blunders and stumbles along always taking, in one form or another, and never producing.

Within the realm of time, space, and casualty, assimilation truly becomes a most ludicrous expression. It is extremely important for us to study and research the original documents (Constitution, Declaration of Independence, Bill or Rights, etc.) with the intent to the interpretation of the Founding Fathers. When certain entities and particular elements, holding fast to and supporting the adopted unit, have conflict with the above documents there will be the inclination to simply ignore, move to accept an abnormal interpretation, justify any non-enforcement, or simply do away with such. To take all in question, the pure intent of the Founding Fathers will force itself upon us with no distortion as in the reality of a nation to which they anticipated and expected. The conglomeration of idiocy which we now call our government pursues the direct opposite of what our Founding Fathers created and fashioned into reality for us (European Americans/Europeans). "The Roman of the Empire ceased to be a Roman through the contemplation of the world that lay at the feet; he lost himself in the crowd of foreigners that streamed into Rome, and degenerated amid the cosmopolitan carnival of arts, worships and moralities" (Nietzsche, 2005, p. 28-29). As European Americans/Europeans, let us not disappear into this multi-ethnic heap produced, given, and driven by the government and its enacted policies.

Let us not follow the destructive and devastating paths of our Roman brothers and sisters.

So, let us be realistic and truthful. The coming together/ joining of multiculturalism and government has produced the vile child of political correctness. These three entities and their created spin-off elements have moved to be the antithesis of European American/Europeanism and what the Founding Fathers envisioned. In regard to America and to what the Founding Fathers imagined as to have created, the question must be posed, who would build a dwelling for those other than his or her own? What people would build a homeland and create a government/regime/system for individuals other than their own? America was put into being for the European American/European and his or her religion. The gist of the above is that the Founding Fathers would not ask more of us than what they, themselves, were prepared to give and did sacrifice.

CHAPTER 8:
THE QUESTION OF MAN
AND EDUCATION

The European American/European child must, in the realm of basic Preschool-6th grade education, learn to read and write well. The basics of mathematics must be adhered to in the development of logic. He or she must adhere to and hold fast to the expression of the English language and languages of Nordic origin. The understanding of other languages will, certainly, be promoted. The child must be a listener. The child should be encouraged to read and write and study his or her interests (that which appeals) at this stage of life. The arts must be learned, considered, and thought upon. Innocence should be the order of the day within this stage of life. The child should have time to think. European Americanism/Europeanism should be studied, deliberated, and reflected upon from the approach of creative thinking, <u>not</u> critical thinking. This will produce a frame of thought to certain intellectualism nourishing a state of mind inspiring self-discipline. Self-discipline (strength of mind/strength of will) will be studied and acquired (realized) and then applied and cultivated to exactness.

Creative thinking must be encouraged with the intangible giving thought to the tangible; thus, ideas leading to achievement. The study of physiology and personal hygiene will be applied on a daily basis. Also, there must be education within the concept of relationship. The male must be cultured and informed to the respect and treatment of the female and the female must be cultured and informed to the respect and treatment of the male. The analysis of the chain of command, authority, self-discipline, and racial awareness will be incorporated into daily study; this is paramount. The overall analysis will pursue concepts of right and wrong. In this environment, the perception of creative thinking must be emphasized in all approaches.

Within education, leading in the preparation as to life, our survival and continued existence will depend on intestinal fortitude (guts), analytical, and creative thinking (logic to communication), and philosophical leadership to direction (racial pride of guidance exhibiting an unwavering loyalty). The great majority of our elites will come from our lower classes (to include the lower-lower class) and our middle classes (to include the upper-middle class). The tempering of those individuals will lead to the new salt of the earth. These people will not necessarily be influential or privileged, but they will know how to win and what it takes to win and what is demanded of body and soul to win, and most important they will have the burning desire to win. Our people will want to be alive in the glory of victory. We (European Americans/Europeans) are all gifted in some form or fashion and, so stated, we simply have to tap into that gifted element or the talented domain of each individual for the cause of existence.

We must educate our people to let their racial emotion develop into the intensity of pride and honor and loyalty. The cultivating of discipline to comradeship (camaraderie) is paramount. There is no sense in believing that a person is able to motivate another person. However, there can be the creation of an environment and surroundings where the person intrinsically self-motivates himself or herself. This must be the right environment for the right motivation for our racial existence and, thus, must be the core/quintessence of our educational system. It would be very correct to say the educational system is responsible for the creation of the leader whom through ability/resources, conduct/behavior, and character/integrity applies all of his or her resources to the dedication and preservation of his or her race (European American/European). It would also be correct to state that we desire an ideological leader and, any ideological leader must be grounded into the concept of his or her history for continued strength. "Only strong personalities can endure history; the weak are extinguished by it. History unsettles the feelings when they are not powerful enough to measure the past by themselves" (Nietzsche, 2005, p. 32). Our civilization must be manifested and revealed and continued through our education.

Education must show the racial undertaking. Education and commitment should move together for a purpose within the European American/European. While oratory, debate, and the dialectic approach are important, these items must have foundation and origin for the establishment of dialogue and discourse. The development of the mind toward racial worth and meaning and consequence, is dominant as the physical and the ethical will be established or come into an exact nature at the later date. So, the discipline and the quest for knowledge will move hand in hand. The racial educational process, with reference in the sustaining to innocence within the child, will take precedence over worldly thoughts and notions. The child must be exposed to the European American/European racial thought of education from birth forward and onward. Let us be meticulous in preparing the future of our race.

We must establish, recognize, sustain, and support alternative forms of education (various, non-traditional approaches). Honing the elements in developing a final product, offered by a non-traditional approach to education, there should be the coming together of theory, experience, observed action, the on-going accumulating of knowledge to occurrence, etc. I am of the opinion that today's formal education process reflects to a culmination in handling correctly accepted thought and then, regurgitating this particular thought in some form of communication; the final occurrence of running this politically correct gauntlet reflects itself in degrees, certifications, licenses, memberships, etc. True education starts and becomes a fact of life with commitment to his or her racial homeland/populace (what the individual accomplishes within and for his or her racial civilization and culture [formal and non-formal, but all inclusive]). Approaching and within this train of thought, the license does not make the individual, the individual, himself or herself, makes the mark. It would be most acceptable to see more individuals (European Americans/Europeans) practicing education, law, etc. without belonging to the so-called/self-styled professional organizations and minus the fancy licenses (so called door openers).

The initiative of inspiration in representing themselves and their own would challenge the person to flourish. Our racial commitment does practice within and does focus on the person not the paper, the application in addition to the thought, the practical realization in addition to the theory, the tangible not just the intangible, etc. Allegiances leading to and reflecting results, from honor and loyalty and commitment, must rule the day. This is not to downplay the inventiveness, ingenuity, and creativeness which comes of mind in ideas and thinking (for, from thoughts come accomplishments). However, what must happen now develops from actions which are observable in results and the bringing forth of consequences (for even the greatest actor or actress must have the supporting cast or nothing is achieved);

contrary to popular belief, the audience is not mandatory for a perfect performance.

With this being said we must revisit traditional institutions which have put us (European Americans/Europeans) in the mess we are surrounded by and now facing (to be most explicit, racial extinction). The educational system is one of these traditional institutions.

So, all of the above must be intertwined within the chain of command, respect for authority, personal self-discipline, and complete racial awareness. This will be incorporated within a daily pursuit as the approach and attitude to life.

CHAPTER 9:
THE QUESTION OF
MIND AND MATTER

The mind influences matter through racial awareness. What the person (European American/European) is, certainly, does happen to sway and inspire the attitude in affecting and inspiring the shaping of matter. The effecting of matter must follow. Mind and matter happen to be the sustaining elements of racial existence. That which inspires the soul addresses the approach to and the reality of racial life. The mind motivates and the matter accomplishes with the combination representing the will to outcome and result. The key is the stabilization to growth of the racial needs (racial life [the one to the family and the family to the one]) as the motivation of mind to matter.

For the ability of mind and matter to function, let us approach the situation from a certain standpoint. There must be the creation/coming about of mind and matter. So, mind and matter do not necessarily stand alone, but encompass or bring together the reality of the Creator (God). This would give reason in answer to the question of which was in existence at the first: the mind or the matter? Within this certain standpoint, the perception would be that both were created at the same time. Now, the psyche does easily fit into the mind as the matter belongs to the brain. So, the mind tells us why we accomplish and the brain shows us how the accomplishment is achieved/is to be done/attained (the intangible translates to the reality of the tangible). For us, the common denominator is race (such always has been, is, and always will be). The Godly and divine blessing is our race, or such would not be so. Belief, trust, and reason exist from the coming together or combination of mind and matter. The mind and the matter act as one for the race (European American/ European). Reality is composed of the now and the preparation therein. The blest mind and the blessed/ consecrated matter combine to become the racial being of awareness and substance for triumph of racial deed; if such were not so, then such would not be.

Within mind and matter, incorporating racial existence and ethnic being, the concept of the European American/European fraternal war and the reasons for such must be forever eliminated. The rationale for incitement and provocation must be done away with (abolished) to include that outside influence with regard to manipulation and agitation. To this end, there must be the rising above the act of human nature which leads to internal strife in a power struggle. Internal strife must be surmounted at all costs or we shall lose our existence. What purpose does it benefit a leader to become the captain of naught? The old maxim of every man has his price must move to become null and void; thus, our Model should become a function of the mind and matter to/within being. "In this spiritualized form, fame is something more than the sweetest morsel for our egoism; in Schopenhauer's phrase it is the belief in the oneness and continuity of the great in every age, and a protest against the change and decay of generations" (Nietzsche, 2005, p. 14). I am of the belief that internal strife may be quelled and controlled through leadership as to a chain-of-command to facilitate the delegation of authority, honor to loyalty, and the power of the will (racial intent to racial interpretation/ethnic intent to cultural interpretation).

So, within mind and matter this ethnic existence and cultural life must be defined as racial nationalism (Euro-Americaneuropeanism). At this point, racial nationalism becomes the common denominator. Wars should be fought for one purpose only: the advancement to or the protection of our race (European American/ European). Wars and/or police actions for many decades leading to years upon years have been fought for non-racial agendas or for the wrong purposes altogether. Such conflicts are a waste of time and energy from the European American/European perspective and should be shunned, avoided, and rejected (such conflicts simply do not benefit us). We need to move beyond superficial points and react to the crux of the issue: our European American/European race, no more and no less (this is the exact summation of the issue). Good or bad, right or wrong, correct or incorrect, obedience or disobedience, etc. must be measured and assessed by a cultural, religious approach (spiritual) to perception and by a cultural, secular viewpoint (temporal) to a racial perspective (Euro-Americaneuropeanism). I am saying, within the above arrangement, complete mind and complete matter are motivated to the identical and are not opposite one another. Euro-Americaneuropeanism is the way of approaching a survival to existence and in the living of life. Pure racial aptitude and intellect are given by God (the Creator) to the mind and the matter. *Alea iacta est* (the die is cast) within this attitude and thus, must be undertaken. For the European American/ European, this approach and method has been, is, and will be (must apply in practice) implemented for our existence.

Within mind and matter, racial nationalism is not defined by blood and iron, blood and language, blood and country, etc. but by blood, mind, and religion. This puts in force a basic enthusiasm to loyalty of camaraderie with a deriving or obtaining in purpose from the temporal and the spiritual viewpoint. Such is very important to realize, as the above statement is quite demanding in racial purpose to individual application and personification: The concepts may be as simple as child's play in understanding or as difficult as the universe to comprehension and are the products of function to total devotion. The mind thinks and the matter must accomplish thus, coming together as the power of the will (the individual Model) representing the justification and rationalization through spirituality. The European American/European must perceive, in the positive application, to exist.

The end justifies the means through the blood (ethnic group/race [of history]) and intellect (racial approach and understanding [values and way of life]) and the belief (faith [spirit and life-force or inner self]). The now and the eternal must be addressed through reason to accomplish that which is beyond revenge, away from envy or greed, and outside of retribution. Created, within racial nationalism, is the intrinsic motivation for living and an all-knowing reason for dying. The observance of action must be justified by the intangible belief of the psyche. So, as the action of matter is accomplished, the mind is set by (rationalized) calmness to harmony (bringing together/fulfillment). All opposing matter must be undertaken with a justified fierceness and, thus, accepted by the confident/self-assured mind. The feats, as yet to be accomplished by the European American/European, will be legion. For the European American/European the above will be our new idealism to confidence (self-assurance, self-belief, self-reliance, self-possession, self-sufficiency, etc. [Euro-Americaneuropeanism]).

CHAPTER 10:
THE QUESTION OF
IDEAS AND THINKING

"What does not kill me makes me stronger"
(Nietzsche, 1990, p. 33).

A s previously stated, there are the major choices, within a lifetime, which probably amount to four or five decisions and the minor choices which do take place everyday. Situations will surround all choices. Now, does the Nietzsche quote above apply? Absolutely. What we come through and experience and survive does not break us but prepares us for the obligation of assignment. "All hard suffering inspired a degree of confidence" (Nietzsche, 1997, p. 16). It tempers us for the task, mentally and physically. It is the mettle of man that matters. And so, ideas and thinking influence the disciplines of life as well as the disciplines of function. The key to the statement leads to purpose (stronger for what, if not reason to determination for purpose [we all have our crosses to bear, it is how we bear them and, also, with what tenacity we approach them]).

Within the above, if such is to be accepted, I would state it is certainly not bad at all to experience that which has the ability to challenge the individual mentally and physically. The above will shake the foundations of an idle and non-purposeful life. The above will agitate and disturb the mind and body to its core existence. That which has the capacity and capability to negatively confront the person both emotionally/psychologically and cruelly/callously may find itself defeated in time, by the person who is sustained by racial application and racial spirituality. The will of man translates to and becomes determination and courage through the experience. The mind may actually speak within itself and state: Dear God, if I can just get through this, I will conquer anything that looms on the horizon. Such becomes the mettle of man.

An approach must reveal that the society becomes the racial and religious reflection complete to those represented people. So, society is nothing more than those which form it and breathe life into it. To interject the foreign body stifles and ruins said societal mechanism for continuation or accomplishment. At this point, the question of why introduce and interject the strange, the unfamiliar, and the unrelated body must be asked of those which have enacted this process/procedure throughout the years (last several decades)?

The idea and thought of giving will certainly be acceptable and welcome. However, altruism and philanthropy are futile unless such (vast amount) happens to be supplied to one's own race. The thought, of continued existence, is to be forthcoming through the exact action of benevolence. These elements enact and put into being within the one/individual and the whole/group a distinct willingness to pursue a manner of unselfishness and self-sacrifice. So, if we do not take care of our own and assist ourselves, it is for sure none of those within the other will. We must help ourselves. I would encourage the taking on of problems directly (head on) as our society only works when we become engaged in all aspects. The above piece deals directly with responsibility and awareness and accomplishment. "Maturity of knowledge, i.e. the degree of perfection to which knowledge can attain in each individual, consists in this, that in every case an exact correspondence has been achieved between abstract concept and perceptual comprehension, so that every concept rests directly or indirectly on a perceptual basis, through which alone it possesses real value, and that every perception can likewise be subsumed under the concept appropriate to it" (Schopenhauer, 1970, p. 231). The key to success is responsibility leading to accomplishment. Awareness, within the individual, is the vehicle to said achievement: as to the positive action moving from one point to another (positive progression). The concept of altruism and philanthropy may be consistent but the individual recipient should and must change or adjust, on a positive basis, as time passes.

Through the past, present, and future actions of experience and observance, formed ideas and creative thinking may show that assimilation will most certainly be of a disadvantage to us (slow eradication). The idea of thought that situations need to be corrected by assimilation is ludicrous. Gross assimilation is not a viable option or acceptable arrangement. Thus said, there are groups we do not want to see incorporated or integrated with the European American/European being.

What one must understand is that ideas and thinking are, and should be, racial in major issues, leading to an ethnic approach within all minor issues. So, these major issues revolve around and influence the lesser issues of daily living (daily involvement of life). Not surprisingly, in the homogeneous society, ideas and thinking are racial. And, not surprisingly, in the heterogeneous society, ideas and thinking are also racial. We simply cannot move away from racial identity within the realm of thoughts and thinking, nor should we try. To contemplate otherwise is mishmash, as one is only fooling himself or herself. Do not be deceived into thinking that life will be much better in the pure multicultural society: Experiences prove otherwise as ignominy seems to be the order of the day for those of European American/European ancestry.

The cultural essence of the European American/European should become the center of his or her racial intelligence (that of the purpose/intention and obsession/enthusiasm). The disciplines of life (true knowledge) are born within this cultural essence. As to the concept thereof, such becomes reality of ideas and thinking (the intent and the interpretation).

Carl von Clausewitz states in his famous aphorism, "War is merely a continuation of policy...by other means" (1998, p. 7). What one must ask himself or herself is the question of just what is policy, and the makeup of such, as per Clausewitz? War, as defined by Clausewitz, may be equated or compared to policy itself. War may very well be the synonym for nationwide policy. In this case, the makeup of policy may be likened with nationalism of country.

So, it is the nationalism of country (e.g., England in war with Germany, Scotland and Ireland in war with England, Canada in war with Germany, Austria in war with Germany, England in war with Russia, France in war with Russia, Australia in war with Germany, New Zealand in war with Germany, England in war with Italy, France in war with Austria, Italy in war with Spain, French Canadians in War with British Canadians, America in war with Germany, England in war with Spain, France in war with England, the British Empire in war with the Austro-Hungarian Empire, the civil wars within Western nations, etcetera, etcetera, etc.) which has plagued and overwhelmed Europe and the European man. Thus, years upon years upon years of European fighting and killing European, for whatever reason, has drastically and severely taken its toll and charge. Unfortunately, the European race may be defined as the ultimate masochist (with regard to punishing and killing itself). An important issue, which must be comprehended, is that nationalism of country is <u>not</u> racial nationalism; the two are not to be compared or equated on a good note (nationalism of country is the antithesis of racial nationalism or Euro-Americaneuropeanism). It is Europe and the European being's alienation of his or her racial thought process(s) (ethnic ideas and cultural thinking) within the disciplines of life which has wrecked havoc on our race for several thousand years. Any anti-European political process or anti-European ideology could not have created a greater enemy for our race than fervent and passionate nationalism of country. However, through the progression of ideas and thinking comes an innovation and knowledge through a consciousness of racial awareness.

Euro-Americaneuropeanism states a process through the progression of ideas and thinking which culminates with the practicing of racial nationalism. Within Euro-Americaneuropeanism, the boundaries of countries fall and racial brotherhood circumvents and precludes these boundaries. Euro-Americaneuropeanism flows within and throughout the disciplines of life to motivate the disciplines of function. The pursuance of ideas and thinking within Euro-Americaneuropeanism produces results (a rational comprehension of knowledge) within the racial Model (European American/European man and woman). Ideas and thinking will not in themselves be an end, nor is any result an ending to outcome in the equation. The culmination of the equation must be the correct and proper result. Euro-Americaneuropeanism is simply the method to the racial Model and is the meshing/coming together, of the "conceptual knowledge" and the "sense knowledge" (Frost, 1989, chap. 10). So, Euro-Americaneuropeanism is our mode and vehicle for existence and with that being said, it is vastly important that Euro-Americaneuropeanism will be our learning process.

Within Euro-Americaneuropeanism, we need to be a bit more particular and precise in asking for and seeking God's blessing. This is particularly true within Christianity as I believe Euro-Americaneuropeanism thrives and flourishes within Christianity and visa versa. Within Euro-Americaneuropeanism, we must embark toward a new era. For us, this is the epitome to/ of ideas and thinking.

Inside the concept of ideas and thinking, within Euro-Americaneuropeanism, the elimination of crisis management (and, the elimination of decisions made within an emotional state of being) is as close to becoming as much of a reality as possible. The most important aspects of survival will be an advanced ability and form of leadership, a mental and physical application of a justified racial attitude in being, and procreation within a progressive racial setting: All else will follow. The following two statements are somewhat inseparable: Eugenics will be, certainly, paramount in the approach to application; the proliferation and procreation within the same racial stock (Nordic racial stock) happens to be most important. At the moment, each statement dwells upon the other. Also, remember, any challenge is judged by the final outcome (i.e., the confrontational situation is only incorrect if one does not win). However, I must be adamant in the comment: There must be guidance to victory. So, circumstances must be directed and controlled (through the correct type of leadership [a process of ideas and thinking]). Now, I state yet again, there is a vast difference in brutality and cruelty. All combined, this will be a confirmation of accomplishment within the being (Model).

Multiculturalism is nothing more than a fancy euphemism for all that is anti-European American/ European (that which is against and opposed to the traditional being). The European American/European must remember, and take quite serious, that within the American multicultural cesspool there are and will be no guarantees of anything to the traditional being (the European American/European individual); this will involve physical violence, mental harassment and psychological abuse, religious mistreatment (persecution), etc. So, multiculturalism would be the antithesis of Euro-Americaneuropeanism.

Let us surmise. Is our racial situation dire? Yes. Is our cultural condition ominous? Yes. Is our societal community of existence threatened? Yes. Is our ethnic condition foreboding? Yes. However, to believe the notion that the *White/European* race has never before experienced the situation which we now face is ludicrous (the circumstances may change but the ultimate danger and menace does not and, actually, never really has). Truly, it must be stated that the European American/

European individual, for many reasons, has only played at existence within life for the last several decades. There has been no meaning of essence/spirit racially or religiously and there has certainly been no racial fervor or passion; that person, of European American/ European ancestry, is not actually living or active as to his or her real self (ethnic nature, racial character, cultural identity, etc.). Within and without/esoterically and exoterically, there have been anti-European American/European entities seeking a purging, suppression, and an outright annihilation; these entities have been pursuing active intimidation and threats to stifle, vigorous forcing, harassment, and a singling out for degradation and disgrace for many years toward and against the European American/European. So, I state, Euro-Americaneuropeanism must be a learning process and awareness that builds upon itself.

We need to unashamedly state our demands (what we will possess, have, and obtain) and then work, diligently, toward these ends:

- We will have an all encompassing worldly brotherhood and nation/land for European Americans/Europeans
- We will have a nation/land with its own autonomy
- We will have a total all encompassing media that, while reporting the truth, will be positive in approach
- We will educate, police, judge, govern, and praise and punish our own

- We will develop our own technology
- We will have our Christianity (unashamedly present [religion])
- We must be racially proactive for the correct racial reaction (there is no need to shriek and cry when no one is available to hear and aide)

While history is extremely important, we do live in the present and often, and at this point, to affix blame is futile as the management of moving forward must be in a positive progress. We will through development, progression, and practice administer our own people. Once put into operation, Euro-Americaneuropeanism will become an entity unto itself with parts in functioning priority for said entity (a going concern underlying cultural principle and ethnic code of belief to a racial order). Euro-Americaneuropeanism in the precise development of technology must flourish and is extremely important.

Ideas and thinking, within Euro-Americaneuropeanism, incorporates and formulates the conceptual, empirical, creative, and intuitive. Empirical circumstances surround a being of ethnic reason and racial intellect, thus, to determine and then develop a norm puts in motion/implies a cultural creative and intuitive thought process of progression to improvement. This norm will constantly be improving and moving forward to become our racial Model. Such will involve a complete racial purpose to not only act but react with positive racial results.

The countries and continents of European descent (America, Canada, Australia, Europe, Russia, New Zealand, and other great areas of European ancestry and parentage [Nordic tribes/Nordic racial stock/Nordic sub-racial stock]) must not only survive but flourish together. I believe the foundation and solution to our survival will be racial camaraderie and have so stated. This must be accomplished within the process of ideas and thinking to the philosophical points so mentioned. The bloody conflicts between our brothers and sisters will be no more. There must be the coming together of the European being and there must be the racial process of learning and moving forward into our future. So, we must look to this brotherhood in the present for the future. "If the judgment of a people hardens in this way, and history's service to the past life is to undermine a further and higher life; if the historical sense no longer preserves life, but mummifies it, then the tree dies unnaturally, from the top downward, and at last the roots themselves wither. Antiquarian history degenerates from the moment that it no longer gives a soul and inspiration to the fresh life of the present" (Nietzsche, 2005, p. 20). Such a brotherhood is already here and at hand but must be cultivated and supported. There are new alliances to be formed and new reminiscences to be made. This is the crux of Euro-Americaneuropeanism.

In Summation:

The above is a practice, at the approach, to existence within the living of life. It is the coming together of the philosophical and the pragmatic for an exact continuation of being (the why and the how). It flows into the culmination of Euro-Americaneuropeanism. The term Euro-Americaneuropeanism is all-encompassing and all-inclusive and a zenith of historical values applying to a certain type individuality (the White racial type relating to the temporal and the spiritual [the complete Euro-Americaneuropeanism mindset]). I state Euro-Americaneuropeanism is the ongoing event resulting from learning and intuitive knowledge and creative thinking.

I would hope the above to be adequately adapted by the European American/European and, therefore, racially guiding. These elements have always been in existence just, often, being relaxed, dormant, or subdued. It would also be my expectation that the above be adopted for further application of thought and reality. The philosophical points were referenced from the book by S.E. Frost, Jr., *Basic Teachings of the Great Philosophers.* My approach encloses, encases, and, hopefully, reveals and relates these 10 basic teachings of the European American/European to a perception and perspective. In this case the European American/European racial core is paramount and overriding (supreme to importance). This must be reality for us.

Even within bleak and dismal circumstances nothing is to be predictable (bound to happen). However, after becoming reality, there can always be the reaction to or manipulation of a situation; but, once again, nothing is inevitable. So, when we are told that such and such is unavoidable or inescapable, actually, just the opposite may be located on the horizon representing very positive results for our race. Our racial instinct and ethnic character assures us of this phenomenon, for is such not our catalyst or binding tie? Any and all effort will be our racial *modus operandi* leading to our complete racial *modus vivendi.*

The person (European American/European) steps out into the universe as a spirit uninhibited within our racial belonging. The inward and outward senses must be keen to this attitude. As to the temporal, with such being said there is the question asked, just what is morality and just what is wickedness? The ultimate of morality is the loving of oneself within one's own (what one is and all that comes with it) and the ultimate of wickedness must be the hating or loathing of oneself and what one is (what one happens to be and all that comes with it). In reality, with whom has nature made the individual most content (to be surrounded by)? So, we must boycott alliances with those other than our own. This would involve the historic association within the temporal and the spiritual.

The European American/European should apply mind and matter to accomplish goals and achieve plans (racially, to do what it takes) within an organized manner. This statement is simple enough as such focuses upon the commitment to a positive racial understanding. The person, who is not pursuing this commitment (whether consciously or unconsciously), will be a defector and fugitive unto himself or herself for there will be no fulfillment to the nature and identity of the being. Now, a question which begs an answer and demands thought from the European American/European self asks, just what is America? America is the European American/European individual leading the European American/European community (the complete family sphere of identification). If we attain any answer but that of the above, then a true study of an America of the past, the present, and to the future is in order. America is the European American/European idea. America is more than just a meshing of bodies. To be an American reflects a certain individual, a certain way of facing life, and a certain way of living life. Our America is the soul to life of the European American/European. When this soul ceases to exist, at that time, so will the essence of America cease to exist.

Were the European American/European Founding Fathers God-Fearing individuals from a racial approach? One would have to agree that these Founding Fathers were God-Fearing in their approach to the founding of America, the founding of government, and racial application. The temporal will always involve the intent and interpretation. The Founding Fathers had every opportunity to do what is now being done racially within our and their country; however, they did not choose to do what is now being ethnically and culturally done to our and their homeland. So, now, one must ask the question, was America founded to be a racially motivated nation and a European American/European homeland; the Mother Country for people of Nordic tribes/Nordic racial stock/Nordic sub-racial stock? The answer given must be, yes. Then, one must ask himself or herself the question, has the European American/European honored the Founding Fathers' wishes and their example? The answer given must be, no.

As to the eventual termination of fraternal, religious wars which have come and gone, it may be that God's planned answer (to end such wars) is by instigating boring, tedious, and tiresome sermons delivered from the pulpit. In dealing with all the requiems, orations, lectures, etc., we find that we should have developed enough self-discipline not to petition the Lord with pleas; unfortunately, such is not the case, for emotion extracts a tremendous toll. The same may be said, with regard, to the questioning of God and the blaming of God and the quarreling with God. For how can one enter into a dialectic discourse with the omnipotent and infinite?

It may truly be stated, we (European Americans/ Europeans) are no stronger than our weakest link from top to bottom; within the ongoing realm and development of certain circumstances such will be tremendously significant and relevant to the final outcome. The European American/European must be a dedicated unit within thought and action. The weakest link does matter and is certainly important. Education and re-education happens to be of the essence and essential with an ongoing sequence of evaluation, advancement, and promotion. Re-education is no more than the encouragement to reality within his or her culture and ethnicity. The encouragement will lead to a positive engagement.

The dedicated and loyal European American/European individual must move away from the person that hates himself or herself and his or her own. The person that loathes his or her culture from the approach and application of past, present, and future deeds and ideas suffers from unrest within the body and soul. Such is of no benefit in this unnatural state and resides within an abnormal condition. There is no value in the detesting of one's own culture. This type of emotional guilt must come to an end. Now, to be positive, there is hope for this type individual; even Odysseus did eventually arrive to his home.

Miscreant and villainy, upon the unit, should be measured as to an attack upon the group (the unit, with all its racial ability, deprived of not being able to contribute and be productive to the whole). When emotion is dispensed with the attack upon and demise of the unit is realism in that said unit will never be replaced. "The body will then vanish; but the space which it occupied still remains, and this it is utterly impossibly to annihilate in thought" (Kant, 2003, p. 4). The idea, which must be instilled, is to attain all objectives from a racial perspective. So, from this application, there will be legitimized activities and acceptable behaviors for performance to a positive conclusion. Revenge, actually, should never be a consideration, as such thrives on emotion and acting within an emotional state is, most always, extremely dangerous and very costly. Also, a Pyrrhic situation must be avoided (the situation where the end does not justify the means [e.g., the victory is too costly and cannot be sustained]). With this being said, the end simply, and most assuredly, must justify the means for the European American/European. Such an approach must be our motivation.

For our continued existence, I would most emphatically lay emphasis on the following main points of application: leadership as to a chain-of-command to facilitate the delegation of authority; honor to loyalty; and, the power of the will (the European American/ European individual [the Model]). The above rests with the core which must be European racial purity (procreation, unashamed racial awareness, being able to throw off the ruse of multiculturalism, the emphasis of our culture to our own, discipline, etc.). For whatever reason, our main adversaries and foremost foes reside within our own race. It is this villainy, located within our own race, which for many reasons wants to drag the European American/European into the abyss of a non-recognizable existence. This is the same individual that initiated and continues the perverted society at present for the twisted sake of distorted principles or as Nietzsche states, "like a man who throws himself from a tower in order to put an end to the unbearable sensation of vertigo" (Nietzsche, 1956, p. 77). These are the turncoats and deserters to our culture and our civilization and our religion (way of life and existence and spirituality). When the time comes, and it will, let us not forget these traitors and their counterparts.

Let us combat the above with a determined chain-of-command to facilitate the delegation of authority, honor to loyalty, and the power of the will. Such will, with application to the past and the present, focus on the future stressing with urgency the innovation to the advancement of astute and incisive technology and the religious awareness for our people. Within this concept, the most innocent and the most civilized must become the most aggressive (to a mentally and physically controlled state within, to reflect without [the concept of self-discipline]). The emphasis and prominence of our people will be summed up in the declaration of racial camaraderie. For existence, this is our reality with the rest to be left in the hands of God.

As time has come and gone, in general and for all-purposes, the fighting amongst ourselves (to usurp the power of rule, to create a dissention of thought, to formulate a deception of the accumulation of more material items, the amassing of money/funds to be the most important motivator at whatever price bar none, and the lust for perceived power at any expense, etc.) and the mixing with other races has lead to a very dangerous situation for our people (the European American/European). With such a state of affairs and set of circumstances, it is noteworthy to observe the diluting and weakening within European American/ European traditions of worth, culture, nature, and religion. For our continued existence, internal fighting and miscegenation must cease (malignant occurrences and unnatural affairs). The first item, that must come to pass, is for the individual to adopt a mindset of honor to loyalty as to the European American/European people and their character. <u>All of the above beliefs should be viewed as a most valuable learning experience and study to perception</u>. At this point, I would interface/ border a quote to the above thoughts from, the Holy Bible, (1994), Luke 10:10-11 which states, "But into whatsoever city ye enter, and they receive you not, go your ways out into the streets of the same, and say, Even the very dust of your city, which cleaveth on us, we do wipe off against you: notwithstanding be ye sure of this, that the kingdom of God is come nigh unto you."

And so, if the person addressed is not receptive then do not worry or bother about him or her. The statement is also adamant and unyielding with reverberations of either being on our side or against our side and not supporting the in-between characterizations or classifications.

I remember an old maxim or cliché which simply states, the partaking of forbidden fruits will lead to terrible jams. Our total European society and our European American nation of America has indulged in forbidden fruits to the point of gluttony: What has become of the European American/European youth, what has become of our religion, what has become of the European American/European family, what has become of the European American/European will to exist and the will to live and be alive as, and with, European Americans/Europeans? For the most part, a resemblance to racial self-control and ethnic self-discipline and cultural Christian religion happens not to be found within our present society. With few exceptions, there is not the observance of discipline or of allegiance or of honor to loyalty with respect to our splendid culture. To say our country of European American/European America is in an extreme and grave racial mess is an understatement. This is the emptiness and meaninglessness we have been given: the non-discipline of our young people, the misreading/misinterpretation of our religion, the destroying of our family unit, the extinguishing of our will to be European Americans/Europeans, etc. Within the present meaningless/illogical society, there has resulted a smothering of our pride and an oppression of our heritage. Within the society of today (the society to which we have been given), absolutely nothing of the European American/European is sacred (revered).

The European American/European should ask the following questions of himself or herself: Where do I come from, what am I to do, and where do I go from here? These are not empty reflections of thought but total commitment and determination. To hold a handful of earth, the European American/European person will arise to reach for the brilliance of the heavens: The handful of earth representing the heritage never to be relinquished; the evidence of reach representing an action in the present scope of faithfulness to duty; and, the brilliance of the heavens representing the blessing forever given to us in racial pride and harmony. At the end, a person must abide by the thought that he or she has done his or her best through the spirit within the blood. Only the individual, in the questioning of himself or herself, will know the true answer: Was I honest and true to my God and was I honest and true to my race? The intertwining of such cannot be dismissed. No more may be asked and if such was done then all has been consummated.

I do not regard the above as our culmination to completion by any means or stretch of the imagination. Such is meant as a powerful and resilient statement of action to racial mind and soul and to racial ideas and thought. European Americans/Europeans should view all of the above as our element of précis (resume, synopsis, summary, etc) and our common denominator. Our summations, with an account to date, become revitalization within Euro-Americaneuropeanism; from the present, it beckons us to our future in the brotherhood of our own. Euro-Americaneuropeanism is our mutual quality, common characteristic, and shared belief.

REFERENCES

Clausewitz, C. (1998). The ecstasy of war. In Barbara
    Ehrenreich.) *Blood rites:*
    Origins and history of the passions of war. New
    York: First Owl Books.

Frost, S. E. (Ed.) (1989). *Basic teachings of the great*
    philosophers. New York: Anchor books.

Hobbes, T. (1989). Mind and matter. In S. E. Frost (Ed.)
    Basic teachings of the great philosophers. New
    York: Anchor Books.

Jung, C. G. (1973). *Synchronicity: An acausal connecting*
    principle. Princeton, NJ: Princeton University
    Press.

Kant, I. (2003). *Critique of pure reason.* Mineola, New
    York: Dover Publications.

Kemp, A. (2006). *March of the titans: A history of the white race.* Burlington, IA: Ostara Publications.

Merriam-Webster's Collegiate Dictionary. (2004). Eleventh Edition. Springfield, Massachusetts: Merriam-Webster, Incorporated.

Nietzsche, F. (1997). *Daybreak: Thoughts on the prejudices of morality.* Cambridge, United Kingdom: Cambridge University Press.

Nietzsche, F. (2006). *Human all-too-human.* Mineola, New York: Dover Publications.

Nietzsche, F. (1956). *The birth of tragedy and the genealogy of morals.* New York: Anchor Books.

Nietzsche, F. (2005). *The use and abuse of history.* New York: Cosimo, Inc.

Nietzsche, F. (1990). *Twilight of the idols/the anti-christ.* New York: Penguin Books.

Parker, J. & Stanton, J. (Eds.) (2003) *Mythology: Myths, legends, & fantasies.* (2003). Willoughby, NSW 2068, Australia: Global Book Publishing.

Schopenhauer, A. (1970). *Essays and aphorisms.* London, England: Penguin Books.

Schopenhauer, A. (2004). *The wisdom of life.* Mineola, NY: Dover Publications.

Schopenhauer, A. (1969). *The world as will and representation.* Mineola, NY: Dover Publications.

Strauss, B. (2006). *The trojan war.* New York: Simon and Schuster.

The Holy Bible, King James Version. (1994). Pradis CD-ROM: Grand Rapids, MI: Zondervan.com.

END